INNER WISDOM

by

Maya Alexis Belluci

London 2011

INNER WISDOM

Published by NLP Gate Ltd trading as Maya Alexis, London, 2011

Copyrights © © NLP Gate Ltd

Illustrations Anna Stankiewicz

Illustrations copyrights © NLP Gate Ltd

All rights reserved. No part of this publication may be reproduced, stored in a retrieval system, or transmitted, in any form or by any means, electronic, mechanical, photocopying, recording, or otherwise, without the prior written permission of the copyright owner.

ISBN 978-0-9569276-0-6

Designed and typeset by Monika Howarth
M3Graphic Art&Design Studio, Haslingden

Printed by Euro Print, 14 Hanover St, London, W1S 1YH, United Kindom

This book can be ordered direct from the author.

Reproductions of the illustrations are available in different formats from the author.

www.mayaalexis.com

For Foster Perry

INNER WISDOM

Touch My Soul	13
Catch The Hum	15
Where Is The Inner Kingdom?	17
Core Issue	19
Essence of Life	20
Liberation	22
Daughter of The Light	25
The Old Lady	29
Haiku	30
Who Cares?	33
Rescue Me	34
Believe Me	37
Tie Your Own Shoe - Lace	38
Transitional Therapy	40
Be Different	42
Two Tips	45
Short Story	47
Thank You	49
Be The Player!	50
Inner Wisdom	53
Insomnia	55
Haiku 2	57
Fix Me Up	58
Stop Moewing	62
Dancing Over The Moon	64
Oops...	67
Law of Attraction	68
Inner Light	71
...	73
Entanglement	74
Hero's Journey	76
(...)	79

Acknowledgements

I would like to take this opportunity to thank:
Foster Perry
Katarzyna Nowicka
Anna Stankiewicz
Wiktor Moszczyński
Monika Howarth

who participated in the birth of this book.
Thank you from my heart!

Author

INNER WISDOM

Maya Alexis Belluci

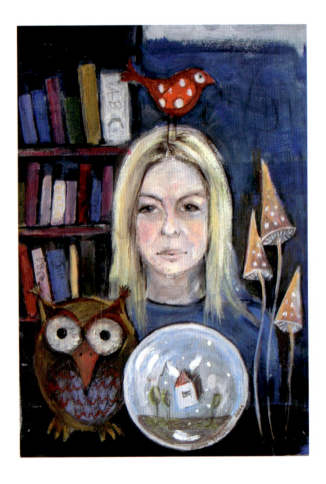

INNER WISDOM

TOUCH MY SOUL

Beauty is a passion
Beauty is a wisdom
Touch my soul
And you know it all

Maya Alexis Belluci

INNER WISDOM

CATCH THE HUM

Catch the hum
Music all around
Birds are singing
Babies crying
Catch the hum

Maya Alexis Belluci

INNER WISDOM

WHERE IS THE INNER KINGDOM?

Channel through
Not from you
Shine it out
Then you know

Maya Alexis Belluci

CORE ISSUE

The grass hooked up with stinky eyes
The telephone rang
Spiraling hurricane creates life path
Nobody answered it
Eternal dimension expands the Beauty Way
Knock, knock to the door
Automatic wash clears your humanity disc
Nobody opened it
Brain Developments immerse in infinite universe
The telephone rang
Torrential rain taps out the camouflage of light
You answered it
Dramatic shadows increase roar of the waves
Knock, knock to the door
Gusts of wind flatten the emotion of life
You opened it
All trauma strings repair the vision of the self

ESSENCE OF LIFE

Glance in the mirror
Can you see
Can you hear
Can you feel
It's your soul
It is you

INNER WISDOM

Maya Alexis Belluci

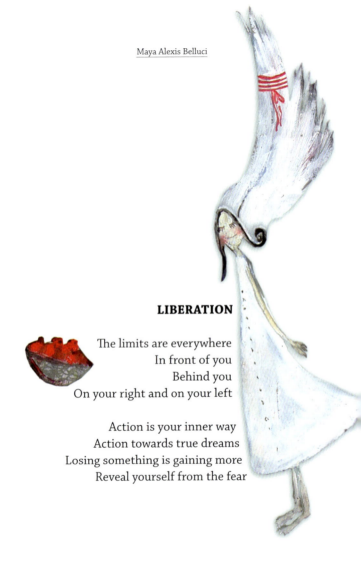

LIBERATION

The limits are everywhere
In front of you
Behind you
On your right and on your left

Action is your inner way
Action towards true dreams
Losing something is gaining more
Reveal yourself from the fear

INNER WISDOM

Maya Alexis Belluci

INNER WISDOM

DAUGHTER OF THE LIGHT

Craziness around me
Imagine what you've done to me
Can you see me
Perfection made you weak to me
Who you are to tell me Lies
Take your disease from my soul
Touch the Devil on your own
I am a Daughter of the Light

WITHIN

Through you
Through light
You find your gun
What do you gonna do ?
LIVE
or
   d
     i
       e

INNER WISDOM

Maya Alexis Belluci

<u>INNER WISDOM</u>

THE OLD LADY

The old lady came into my life
Her inner beauty shone through my heart
Her gentle voice woke me up
She showed me the garden of her soul

HAIKU

The little drop falls from the tree
The baby cries over me
You never find what it is
Your life depends on me

Fool yourself with overdose
Kill your mother and yourself
The Fear comes after you
End finish painting of your past day

INNER WISDOM

Maya Alexis Belluci

WHO CARES?

Sense – gOOd joke!
No sense – really?
   So who cares?
Oh…**you** care!!

Silly you
   Tree of *life*
   Roots of *death*
Everything makes sense

RESCUE ME

Rescue me, rescue me
I am a shit
Yes, you are
Find your way
And then leave

Precious things, precious things
Diamonds, gold
Reach your soul
Feed your greed
And then leave

Goodness – Devil
Where's the link?
Neediness – panic
This is NOT YOUR FAULT
Face it all

INNER WISDOM

Maya Alexis Belluci

BELIEVE ME
Fear is your enemy
Enemy is your good excuse
Fight it, beat it, love it
Fear is your friend

Courage to be what you want
Put courage into words
Courage to be just happy
Put courage into words

Courage to be music
Put courage into words
Courage to be loved
Put courage into words

Words , words, words
Make your essence
Words, words, words
Light your life

TIE YOUR OWN SHOE - LACE
I do not want to please you
I want to be invisible
What you need is not me
What it is… figure it out

INNER WISDOM

TRANSITIONAL THERAPY

Like the motion of the ocean
Like the freedom of worship
Melts the fiction with compassion
Gives a sample of the essence

Open mind
Open the gates of your life
It saves you and your child
Mother, Father follow nature
Challenge the muscles in your mind

Release Excrete Purify

Shake out your love
Jealousy never helps you out
Judgments close you up
Shake out your life

Imagination is released
Feel the story
Imagination is released
Hear the love

INNER WISDOM

Your witch-like nature moulds your soul
Deep transitions force the secrets out
Talk out loud
Louder
Even louder
Burn my mind with the light
Tell me the story of your life
The Mother cell sets out the scene
Welcome conscious neuron into this World
Look through the silent mind

The beauty is aroused in your heart

BE DIFFERENT

Speak up for yourself

speak up for tolerance

Speak up for nature

speak up for innocence

Perfection...bullshit

Cruelty is real

Be different

...or just die

INNER WISDOM

INNER WISDOM

TWO TIPS

Life is Beauty
Don't miss out
Death is Power
Don't find out

Maya Alexis Belluci

INNER WISDOM

SHORT STORY

Once upon a time there was a little girl

Her name was Shame

One day she met Him

His name was Light

She changed her destiny

She discovered the real purpose of Life

Her name was Wisdom now

Maya Alexis Belluci

...

THANK YOU

Thank you Mother
Thank you Father
You taught me loads of things
Mother – how not to be happy
Father – how not to believe in me
But you both gave the most important thing

L
i
f
e

Thank you from my heart

Maya Alexis Belluci

BE THE PLAYER!

Who knows the rules

Can make you happy

Who knows the rules

Can make you messy

Learn the lesson of your life

Be the player of your drive

INNER WISDOM

Maya Alexis Belluci

INNER WISDOM

Whistle in the dark
Anxiety in the body
He is coming from inside
The Devil of your shadow

A sudden drop of the light
Shivers to the muscles
The power of love
The Angel makes a move

Human nature fights them both
Ancient knowledge grips the game
Mystery finds the seed elsewhere
Huge surprise clouds empty eyes

Emotion's river takes a lead
Once you are in there is no escape
Evil, Good lose their sense
Brighter future takes your breath away

Maya Alexis Belluci

INSOMNIA

Special sleep exists in your hidden dream
Humble motion of your soul with the storm
Fear tries to take a lead on your thoughts
Restless genius struggles to find repose

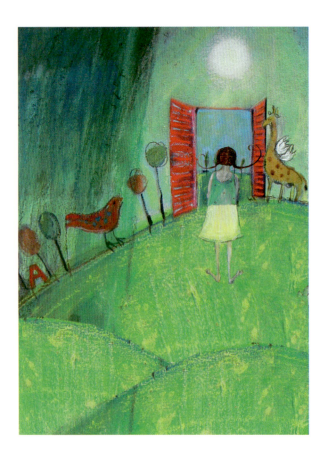

HAIKU 2

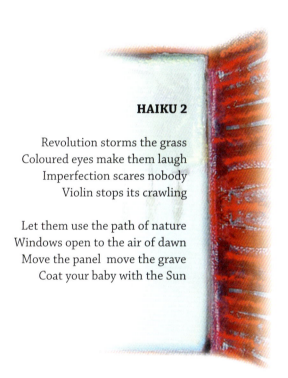

Revolution storms the grass
Coloured eyes make them laugh
Imperfection scares nobody
Violin stops its crawling

Let them use the path of nature
Windows open to the air of dawn
Move the panel move the grave
Coat your baby with the Sun

FIX ME UP

My life is crap
Nobody loves me
Fix me up
  My life is a grave
  Nobody wants me
  Fix me up
    Your life is crap
    You deserve it
    Fuck you
      Your life is a grave
      You chose it
      Fuck you

INNER WISDOM

Maya Alexis Belluci

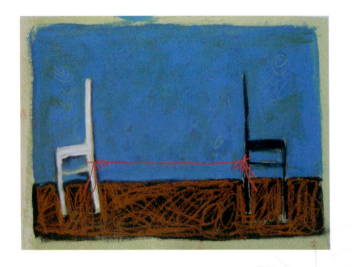

NASTY LOVE

Aggression, compassion
Bonds You tied
No escape
Fear, neediness
Blocks all action
No hope

One way out
Break the link

STOP MOEWING

Time
No time

Nice
Not nice

Let the bullshit come out now

INNER WISDOM

DANCING OVER THE MOON

You meant to be colourful
Like a crystal
Whenever you go
Whatever you do
Bring your soul over the Moon

INNER WISDOM

Maya Alexis Belluci

INNER WISDOM

oops...

Tic Toc, *Tic* Toc, *Tic* Toc

Hurry, hurry, hurry...

Tic *Toc*, Tic *Toc*, Tic *Toc*

oops... the gate is closed

You missed your chance

Maya Alexis Belluci

LAW OF ATTRACTION

There was a man and his dreams
His head over the clouds

There is an empty room and white walls

He walked in and brought out his dreams
With his passion and his love
He stepped out
and discovered the beauty of his life

INNER WISDOM

Maya Alexis Belluci

<u>INNER WISDOM</u>

INNER LIGHT

Kiss my ass
Suck my tit
Bully my mind
And walk away

Ego follows truth of God
Child's laughter blossoms in the air

Inner light comes to life

Maya Alexis Belluci

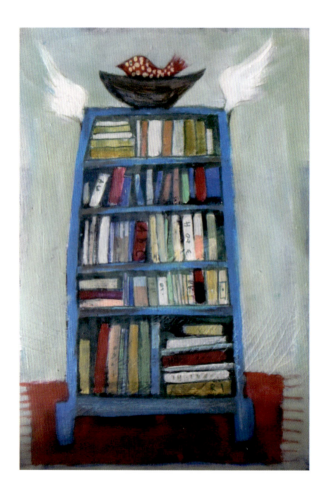

INNER WISDOM

...

Life's rhythm takes the breath away
Holds your passion once in a while
Transforms your body into shadow
Marvellous spirits enrich your sorrow

The beauty lies in a crowded room
Stop lamenting for your genius
Trust your guts and plant the bushes
Take the oxygen to crown your Victory

ENTANGLEMENT

Mother and Son met God
Let me tell you something true

He is not your husband
She is not your wife
Find the real one

Through the ages
Through time
Love tries to find its other half

INNER WISDOM

Maya Alexis Belluci

HERO'S JOURNEY

Hero's journey starts right now
You are Father, you are Son
Frosty jungle makes you brave
Millennium reveals the new feminine side of you
Degeneration must end now
Retrieve male initiation rites from yore
Fast car shortens your healthy heart
Be a Man, be a Power for your Son

INNER WISDOM

Maya Alexis Belluci

INNER WISDOM

(...)

Bless your body with a kiss
Just one tone
Find the spirit to recover life
Just one drop
Candle music in your veins
Just one note

Romancing poetry of God
This is it!

your notes...

Maya Alexis

Discover more about Maya Alexis' poems
and other products online at www.mayaalexis.com